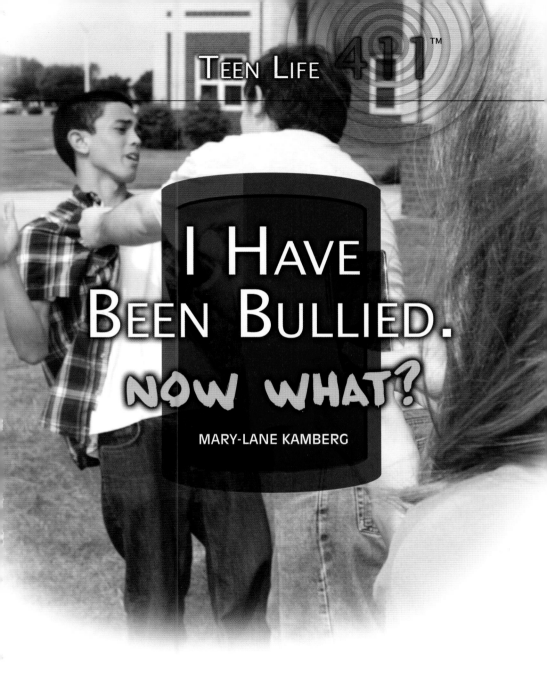

I HAVE BEEN BULLIED.

NOW WHAT?

MARY-LANE KAMBERG

ROSEN
PUBLISHING®

New York

For Luke Anderson

Published in 2015 by The Rosen Publishing Group, Inc.
29 East 21st Street, New York, NY 10010

Library of Congress Cataloging-in-Publication Data

Kamberg, Mary-Lane, 1948–
I have been bullied. Now what?/Mary-Lane Kamberg.—
First edition.
     pages cm.—(Teen life 411)
Includes bibliographical references and index.
ISBN 978-1-4777-7978-1 (library bound)
1. Bullying. 2. Bullying—Prevention. 3. Bullying in schools—
United States. 4. Bullying in schools—United
States—Prevention. I. Title.
BF637.B85K36 2015
302.34'3—dc23

                                        2014010438

Manufactured in China

CONTENTS

President Barack Obama knows what it's like to be bullied. Bullies tormented him as a child. "I have to say, with big ears and the name that I had, I was not immune," he said in a speech at the March 2011 White House Conference on Bullying Prevention reported by CNN. "I didn't emerge unscathed."

In the same speech, Obama said, "If there is one goal of this conference, it is to dispel the myth that bullying is just a harmless rite of passage or an inevitable part of growing up."

Bullying may not be inevitable, but it certainly is common. According to JMGProductions, Inc., which produced the Listen to Our Voices Anti-Bullying Campaign in 2011, 21 percent of U.S. elementary schools, 43 percent of middle schools, and 22 percent of high schools had reported bullying incidents. According to the Bully Project, a social action campaign aimed at putting an end to bullying, more than thirteen million American kids are annually bullied at school, on the bus, in neighborhoods, online, and on

As a child, future U.S. president Barack Obama, shown here at the age of nine with his mother, stepfather, and stepsister, was bullied by his peers.

their cell phones. It is the most common form of violence directed at America's youth.

In its purest sense, bullying is intentional, repeated behavior meant to achieve power or control over another person. Many different types of bullying exist. Examples include verbal, physical, social, and sexual, as well as cyberbullying, which uses electronic media to torment others. In most cases, the target must deal with more than one kind of agony.

No one is safe from bullying. Everyone involved suffers consequences because of it—not only the kid who is bullied, but also the one doing the damage. Negative effects even happen to a kid who simply witnesses the incident. At times, the result is deadly. Understanding the three-way dynamic among bullies, bullied, and bystanders is a first step in stopping the behavior.

Another step is to understand what contributes to the behavior, as well as society's seeming acceptance of it. Experts blame a variety of culprits, such as inborn traits from genetic inheritance, alcohol abuse by a pregnant mother, and domestic or child abuse. Media gets a share of the blame, too, from violent movies, television shows, and video games. Lastly, peers, schools, parents, and communities play a role, either by ignoring or appearing to approve of the behavior.

Targets, peers, and schools have tried a variety of ways to deal with bullying. Many have proven ineffective. However, that dynamic is changing as individuals and organizations work to build awareness of the effects of bullying and study its causes and possible remedies. Some of these efforts have helped build bullying prevention programs now in effect in school districts in the United States, Canada, and elsewhere in the world.

In short, bullying has become a society-wide issue with long-term effects. Stopping it will require long-term commitments from individuals, schools, communities, and other organizations.

CHAPTER 1

WHAT IS BULLYING?

In September 2013, twelve-year-old Rebecca Sedwick killed herself by jumping off a silo at an abandoned cement plant in Lakeland, Florida. Her mother blamed at least fifteen classmates for relentless bullying that she said contributed to the girl's suicide.

The bullying began in November 2012, when a former friend targeted Rebecca because they were both interested in the same boy. The initial tension between the two girls grew when the former friend allegedly recruited others to torment Rebecca. According to the Polk County sheriff's office and reported on the CNN wire, the girls used cell phones and other electronic devices to send her such messages as:

"nobody cares about u"
"i hate u"
"you seriously deserve to die"

That December, Rebecca was hospitalized after slitting her wrists. In response, school

About a month after twelve-year-old Rebecca Sedwick plunged to her death to avoid more bullying, two girls who had bullied her were arrested for "aggravated stalking." Charges were later dropped.

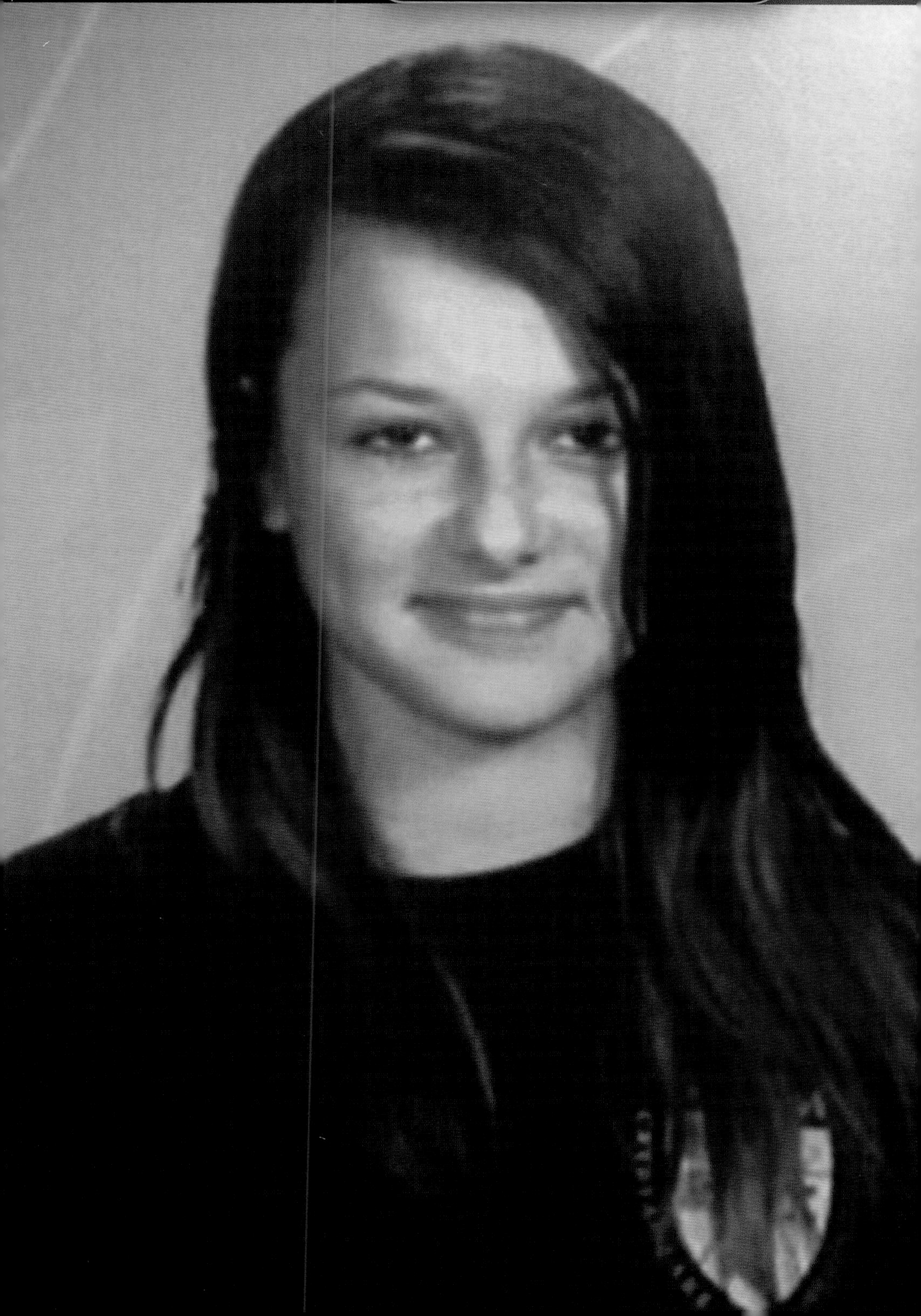

Bullies use texting and other Internet activities as effective weapons against their targets. Victims often live in fear in their own homes because they cannot escape the bully's reach.

officials began an anti-bullying program. Still, nearly a year later, Rebecca sent her own message to a boy she met on Facebook. The night before she died, she said, "I'm jumping. I can't take it any more."

DEFINING BULLYING

Bullying is unwanted, aggressive behavior aimed at harming or controlling another person. At best, bullying causes hurt feelings. At worst—in extreme examples—it causes death. Boys and girls who bully think they are better than those they bully. It's all about dislike, contempt, or outright hatred of someone the bully considers worthless or inferior.

A child who bullies has—or seems to have—some type of advantage over a target. Bullying occurs when a real or imagined power imbalance exists between school-age children. The power imbalance may result from better physical strength, more popularity, or access to embarrassing information. Examples of bullying behavior include taunting, pushing, hitting, tripping, yelling, making threats, spreading rumors, and excluding a victim from a group. Bullying usually is repetitive—or at least has the potential of recurring.

BULLY, THE MOVIE

The feature-length documentary *Bully* was the first film to show the real-life effects of bullying. Originally titled *The Bully Project*, the film opens on the first day of school and covers a year in the lives of kids and parents who each represent a different side of the bullying epidemic. Director Lee Hirsch, who himself was bullied as a child, shot the footage in 2009 in five cities in Georgia, Iowa, Mississippi, and Oklahoma.

The documentary was first shown on April 23, 2011, at the Tribeca Film Festival in New York City. However, the original R rating for language from the Motion Picture Association of America prevented minors from seeing it without a parent. An online petition with more than three hundred thousand signatures, along with the filmmaker's elimination of much of the profanity, resulted in a new PG-13 rating.

Since its U.S. release, it has been shown in Australia, Brazil, Canada, Finland, Germany, Greece, Iceland, Italy, Japan, the Netherlands, Norway, the Philippines, Sweden, and Switzerland.

With an estimated production budget of $1.1 million, the film had grossed more than $4 million in the United States alone by November 2012, according to the IMDb film database. It was released on DVD and Blu-ray on February 12, 2013.

The award-winning film inspired a social action campaign called the Bully Project. The national movement hopes to end bullying in America. Its goal is to reach more than ten million kids. As a start, its "1 Million Kids" program

Students at White Station Middle School in Memphis, Tennessee, view film clips from the feature-length documentary *Bully* during a school assembly led by director Lee Hirsch.

has brought screenings of the documentary to more than a quarter of a million students and 7,500 educators in 120 cities. The program also provides training and an education plan to aid teachers in student discussions about developing empathy and taking action against bullying.

Most incidents occur in the school building during or just before or after school. It also happens on playgrounds, school buses, and routes kids walk to and from school. In fact, bullying can happen anywhere, particularly in neighborhoods and on the Internet. Bullying behavior most often occurs when no adults are present.

The U.S. Department of Justice says younger students are more likely to be bullied than older students, but the type of bullying changes as kids grow older. The National Association of School Psychologists reports that physical bullying increases in elementary and middle school and decreases in high school, but verbal bullying, like mean taunting and putdowns, continues throughout all grades.

An American Medical Association (AMA) study of fifteen thousand students in grades six through ten estimated that 3.7 million youths annually bully others. The National Association of School Psychologists says that between 15 percent and 30 percent of students are either bullies or targets.

The fact is that most kids play some part in bullying activity. They bully or get bullied. Or they witness the behavior. Some kids play different roles at different times.

ARROGANCE IN ACTION

The two main types of kids who bully are those who are well-connected to their peers and those who are isolated from them. Well-connected bullies find popularity extremely important. They enjoy social power and like to control and dominate others. They also like to use others to get what they want.

Isolated bullies may suffer from anxiety or depression. They have low self-esteem and are easily swayed by peers. They blame, criticize, and lie about others as a way to put their own poor traits onto others. However, this type of bully may project an air of superiority to cover up his or her own inadequacies.

All kids who bully share many of the following characteristics. Their main concerns are their own needs, wants, and feelings. They have a hard time understanding others' emotions or respecting basic human rights. They can't empathize with others or view circumstances from another's angle. They may

WHEN KIDS WHO BULLY GET CAUGHT

A kid who bullies seldom takes responsibility for the bullying behavior. If caught in the act by an adult, he or she typically reacts in one or more of these ways:

- Says he or she did nothing wrong

- Says it was just "in fun"

- Criticizes the target

- Blames the other kid for starting it

- Accuses the target of being the bully

- Counts on—or threatens—witnesses to support his or her version of events think of weaker or younger kids as their prey. They also crave attention. They are easily frustrated and have aggressive personalities. They see nothing wrong with violence. In some cases, their parents pay little attention to them, or their home life may be troubled. Often they think bullying will help them fit in, and it's not uncommon for them to find friends who also bully others.

Kids who bully seldom take responsibility for their actions or consider the potential short-term, long-term, or unintended results of what they do. They think they have a right to abuse, control, or dominate others. In their minds, someone who is different from them is automatically inferior. So they have no tolerance for any variation from the norm. They also feel free to exclude others for whom they have no respect or concern.

TARGETS

A child who is the target of bullying stands out as different from others in some way. Some examples include being younger, being fat or exceptionally skinny, wearing braces or glasses, wearing clothes that aren't "cool," being new at school, practicing a particular religion, coming from a certain national origin, being a specific race, having a disability, or having a minority sexual orientation. In some cases, they are targets because their behavior annoys, provokes, or antagonizes their peers.

The differences may also be such positive characteristics as being smart, good-looking, rich, or accomplished in art, dance, music, or sports. No matter what the specific difference is, in the eyes of the bully, the target seems unable or unwilling to defend himself or herself.

INNOCENT BYSTANDERS?

Kids who witness bullying fall into several groups, depending on the role they play when the behavior

Not-so-innocent bystanders often make videos of bullies in action. Some later post them on YouTube, Facebook, or other social media sites.

happens. Their reactions define them. Here are some examples:

- **Tagalongs:** Individuals who don't start a bullying episode, but who join right in when one starts.

- **Supporters:** Individuals who don't participate but who agree with the person who bullies; supporters may even laugh or cheer on the abuse.

- **Closet supporters:** Individuals who like to watch but remain silent.

- **"Not my problem" witnesses:** Individuals who watch but stay out of it.

- **Closet defenders:** Those who don't like the bullying but do nothing about it.

- **Defenders:** Those who stand up for the target, try to calm down the situation, help the target get away from the bully, and/or comfort the target after the event.

The reactions of supporters, closet supporters, and "not my problem" witnesses often contribute to the problem. For instance, someone who doesn't lead the bullying but joins in once it starts encourages the activity. Someone who laughs or cheers provides

an audience and rewards the person doing the bullying. Individuals who hold themselves apart from the
bullying again encourage the bully by not taking a
stand. Their inaction amounts to approval in the bully's mind.

Closet defenders may want to help but don't know
how. Or they may fear that getting involved will mean
they will become the next target. They may be friends
with the bully and not want to lose the friendship.
On the other hand, if the target is not a friend, the
bystanders may see no reason to get involved. They
may be afraid to become associated with the target
and thus lose whatever status they have among peers.
Or they don't want to break the "code of silence" and
get someone in trouble.

Only defenders actually take steps to stop the bullying behavior. They may not always succeed, but they
often make a huge difference in the target's—and the
bully's—life.

IT'S SO EASY BEING MEAN

Bullies have devised a wide variety of ways to be mean to others. The five main types of bullying include verbal, physical, social, sexual, and cyber abuse.

Verbal bullying involves words—oral or written. Verbal bullying ranges from name-calling and taunting to actual threats of harm. The old playground rhyme "Sticks and stones will break my bones, but names will never hurt me" is one of the myths of childhood. Names hurt—inside, where it matters. Verbal bullying also includes exclusion from a group or other consequences if the target fails to comply with the bully.

I WAS ONLY TEASING

Good-natured teasing among friends doesn't qualify as bullying. Teasing has no intent to hurt anyone. It's light-hearted and meant in fun. The teaser and the person being teased easily exchange roles. And if one party objects or becomes upset, the teasing usually stops immediately.

Taunting, on the other hand, is mean. It mocks someone the bully dislikes or even hates. As with other types of bullying, taunting involves an imbalance of power. It is one-sided and always directed toward the target. Taunting uses humiliating or bigoted comments often masquerading as jokes. If the person on the receiving end objects or reacts with anger or tears of frustration, the taunting continues or increases.

BODILY HARM

Physical bullying involves hurting a person's body or damaging his or her possessions. Physical bullying includes such behavior as spitting, hitting, kicking, punching, tripping, pushing, locking someone in a room

Physical bullying often draws a crowd of onlookers, but other types of bullying occur when no one else is around—or over social media, where victims cannot defend themselves.

or restroom stall, or holding him or her to the ground. It also includes hand gestures and threats of physical harm. Kids who use physical bullying might steal lunch money, throw books, dump out a purse or backpack, or break someone's things.

Physical bullying happens over and over and often gets worse. It may start with a little physical pain but may soon lead to serious injury—or death. Scratches, bruises, bloody noses, and broken bones can result. Threats of future assaults often precede or follow the attacks, so the target lives in fear even when outside the bully's presence.

Adults often confuse physical bullying with "normal" roughhousing. However, it's easy to tell the difference. Playing keep-away with someone's hat where the hat's owner is a willing participant is not the same thing as doing it with the goal of humiliating or upsetting him or her. It's the difference between being all in fun and being intimidating. Adults who ignore bad behavior encourage kids who bully to continue their actions.

In the past, boys more frequently engaged in physical bullying than girls. But today, girls are just as likely to push someone into a locker or stuff her into a trash can as boys are.

So-Called Friends

Social bullying includes purposefully leaving someone out, spreading rumors, telling others not to be friends with someone, and making fun of someone in public.

It affects the target's reputation or turns friends against each other. As with other types of bullying, it is intentional and repetitive.

Kids who practice social bullying ignore, isolate, exclude, or shun a peer. They leave the target off of invitation lists to birthday parties, slumber parties, or other group activities. They fail to include the target in playground games or teams. These kinds of actions often go unnoticed by adults or other kids.

In some cases, a former close friend tells others secrets the target once confided in him or her. Or a person who bullies exaggerates something that happened to reflect negatively on the target. Telling outright lies meant to put the target down is another technique included in this type of bullying. So is repeating something known to be untrue.

Social bullying also includes such open acts as stares, sighs, frowns, sneers, and other body language aimed at causing fear or shame. It also includes playing so-called jokes or pranks on the target and actions meant to break up romantic couples. Spreading rumors or enlisting other kids to join in against a target happens behind the target's back and is noticed only after the fact.

Girls more often use this type of bullying than boys. Unlike targets of other types of bullying, targets of social bullying are likely to be within the circle of friends, who then turn on one of their members. It's usually a group effort, where many kids join together to bully the same target.

Some acts of bullying are crimes. The Fresno County district attorney announces charges against University of California, Fresno, fraternity members in the hazing, alcohol-poisoning death of Philip Dhanens as his parents look on.

Hazing is another type of social bullying. Hazing is a ritual used to initiate newcomers into a group or club. Hazing ranges from silly, embarrassing acts to potentially deadly ones. It was once considered acceptable behavior in high schools, college fraternities, sports teams, and even adult organizations. However, after some hazing resulted in serious injury and death, the practice no longer enjoys universal acceptance as a way to behave.

SPEAKING OF SEX

A particular type of social bullying is known as sexual bullying. It includes both verbal and physical actions. Verbal sexual bullying, like other types of bullying, is based on a power imbalance. It aims to give the person who bullies control or domination of the target. Verbal sexual bullying is one-sided and intended to hurt feelings or injure self-esteem by using demeaning names or comments. If the target reacts negatively, the bullying behavior continues or escalates. Verbal sexual bullying can easily turn into threats or actual physical or relationship abuse.

Verbal sexual bullying includes inappropriate name-calling or comments about gender or sexual orientation. The derogatory terms used differ for boys and girls. Boys get accused of being sissies. Comments like "You throw like a girl" are aimed at demeaning a boy's gender image. For girls, comments about their bodies may include "fat," "ugly," or worse, obscene terms.

Both boys and girls may suffer from name-calling and other comments if they vary from gender stereotypes. For example, stereotypical ideas about boys say that those who are artistic, musical, nonathletic, or sensitive aren't masculine. In the past, girls who were good at sports were considered unfeminine. Today, however, as more girls participate in athletics, this stereotype has lost most of its impact.

Verbal sexual bullying is often directed against kids or teens who are or just "seem to be" lesbian, gay, bisexual, or transgender. Sexist or sexual jokes can also qualify as verbal sexual abuse. So can comments about sexual activity or lack of sexual activity.

Middle school and high school students are particularly vulnerable to this type of bullying because they are experiencing the physical and emotional effects of puberty and are coming to recognize their sexual identity.

Some dating situations fall under the heading of sexual bullying. Such activities as ignoring the dating partner's opinion, talking about sex as if it's a game, or constantly calling to see where the partner is and whom he or she is with count as sexual bullying. So do such physical abuses as beating a dating partner, pressuring or forcing him or her to have sex, or pressuring or forcing unprotected sex. (These also qualify as crimes of assault, battery, rape, or attempted rape.) Among adults, the sexual abuser most often is male, and the target most often is female. Among teens, however, the bully and the target may be either gender in roughly the same numbers.

NET RESULTS

Bullying that uses electronic technology is called cyberbullying. Cyberbullying differs from other types of bullying behavior. For instance, the person who bullies this way often feels a sense of anonymity. Internet messages often are crueler and more vicious than other types of attacks.

According to SaveTeenRapp.org, approximately 50 percent of all youth have experienced some form of cyberbullying, and between 10 percent and 20 percent of them experience repeated, regular incidents of it. These activities include mean texts or e-mails; rumors sent electronically or posted on blogs, chat rooms, or social networks; fake profiles that are meant to humiliate a target; as well as embarrassing images, videos, or posts on websites. A cyberbully might also steal a target's identify and pose as the target to invite people to a nonexistent party—or worse.

Bullies also use the Internet to damage a target's reputation or sexually harass him or her. In addition to run-of-the-mill insults, some cyberbullies have used Photoshop or other software programs to doctor images in a sexual way. Others post fake messages from the target on websites seeking sexual partners and put the target in real-life danger. If a boyfriend-girlfriend relationship goes bad, one partner may post "sexting" images or messages that were intended to be private. (So don't send any!)

Targets have little chance of avoiding the bully. The attacks occur any time of day or night, including during weekends, holidays, and summer breaks from school. It happens anywhere the target accesses the Internet—even in his or her home, where the target should be able to feel safe. Many such targets report feeling trapped by the situation.

Sometimes cyberbullying takes the form of a message sent directly to the target. Other times it comes as an indirect attack. Indirect attacks are attacks made by another person on behalf of the bully. (Of course, this indirect messenger then becomes a bully, too.) Indirect attacks can come from persons who visit a chat room or other site who don't know either the original bully or the target but who join in the "fun." This type of bullying is called "proxy" bullying because one person acts in place of another.

Cyberbullies use social media to terrorize or humiliate their victims in the relative anonymity of the Internet. Sometimes complete strangers participate in bullying in chat rooms.

Cyberbullies can post messages and images on such social media networking sites as Facebook and Twitter and instantly reach a huge—sometimes international—audience before the target even knows about it. Too, once something is posted and distributed, the damage is done—even if the posts are later taken down.

While information in cyberspace reaches many people, the effects often go unseen. Frequently, the target says or does nothing to indicate how much the behavior hurts and distresses him or her.

MYTH:

Bullying is a harmless, inevitable part of growing up.

FACT:

Bullying is neither harmless nor inevitable. In some cases it results in serious harm—or death. Bullying is avoidable. Efforts to build awareness and break the cycle of violence are making a difference.

MYTH:

Bullies are stronger than those they bully.

FACT:

Physical strength is only one type of power imbalance that exists between kids who bully and their targets. The bully's "power" can come from such sources as age, size, academic grades, sports ability, popularity, being a member of a particular race or religion, and more.

MYTH:

Kids who are bullied are weak, insecure loners.

FACT:

Not all kids who are bullied start out weak and insecure. However, that may describe how many appear after long-term, continuous bullying.

MYTHS AND FACTS

CHAPTER 3

WHY DOES BULLYING HAPPEN?

No one is born a bully. Bullying is something a person learns. The main factors that influence why such behavior starts—and why it continues—include inborn traits, defense strategies, family dynamics, media exposure, and community, school, and peer group interactions.

Biological traits can contribute to the making of a kid who bullies or one who becomes the target of a bully. Some babies born with fetal alcohol syndrome—from mothers who abused alcohol during pregnancy—later exhibit poor socialization skills. They have trouble making and keeping friends, as well as getting along in groups.

Children and teens with various social disabilities may become bullies out of inability to understand correct behavior. Because some conditions may make the individual seem different from the "norm," children and teens who have them may become targets of bullies themselves. Or if they aren't targeted first, they might choose to attack before someone attacks them.

Many targets of bullying keep to themselves without openly reacting. However, the internal pain bullying causes can produce anxiety and depression in someone who has no other risk factors.

Someone who is the object of bullying often turns around and bullies others. Since they were bullied and nothing happened to the bully, the targets may sense that such behavior is condoned by their peers, school officials, or the community and is an acceptable way to behave. They may strike out against weaker peers or siblings.

ALL IN THE FAMILY

A child who lives in a family where bullying behavior or outright verbal, emotional, or physical abuse occurs has a good chance of bullying peers. Parents and/or siblings in this situation act as role models for bullies-to-be. Children may suffer from abuse themselves or witness one parent abusing the other. Or an older sibling may be the abuser.

A child who receives negative verbal or physical messages at home is likely to develop low self-esteem. Bullying someone outside the family gives him or her a sense of power and importance. Low self-esteem also contributes to the bully side of the bully-target pairing because bullies usually target someone they perceive as weaker and unlikely to retaliate.

Even families where abuse is absent can affect a child's risk of becoming a bully or target. If the child witnesses inconsistent consequences of bullying behavior, he or she is likely to think bullying will go unpunished.

VIOLENCE ON THE SCREEN

Not all bullies come from unstable families. Other factors are also at work. One is aggressive behavior shown in movies and on television. Another influence may come from violent video and computer games. Ever since the 1980s, researchers have found links between the number of hours a child watches television and such violent, real-life acts as threats, assaults, robbery, and use of weapons.

The link between video games and behavior is even stronger. In one study, two groups of subjects played video games. One game was analytical in nature. It required complex thinking and problem-solving skills. The other was violent; its object was to kill enemies. The two groups then came together, and researchers observed their behavior. The subjects who played the killing game acted more aggressively than those who played the analytical one.

Not everyone who plays such games as *Grand Theft Auto* becomes a serial criminal. However, as recently as 2008, the American Medical Association said that violence in media increases the occurrence of mean-spirited, aggressive behavior. The AMA added that media violence increases fear, mistrust, and self-protective behavior toward others. It also hardens participants to violence, which makes disrespect and aggression seem like an acceptable way to act.

In 2010, the watchdog group Common Sense Media reported the Kaiser Family study that said

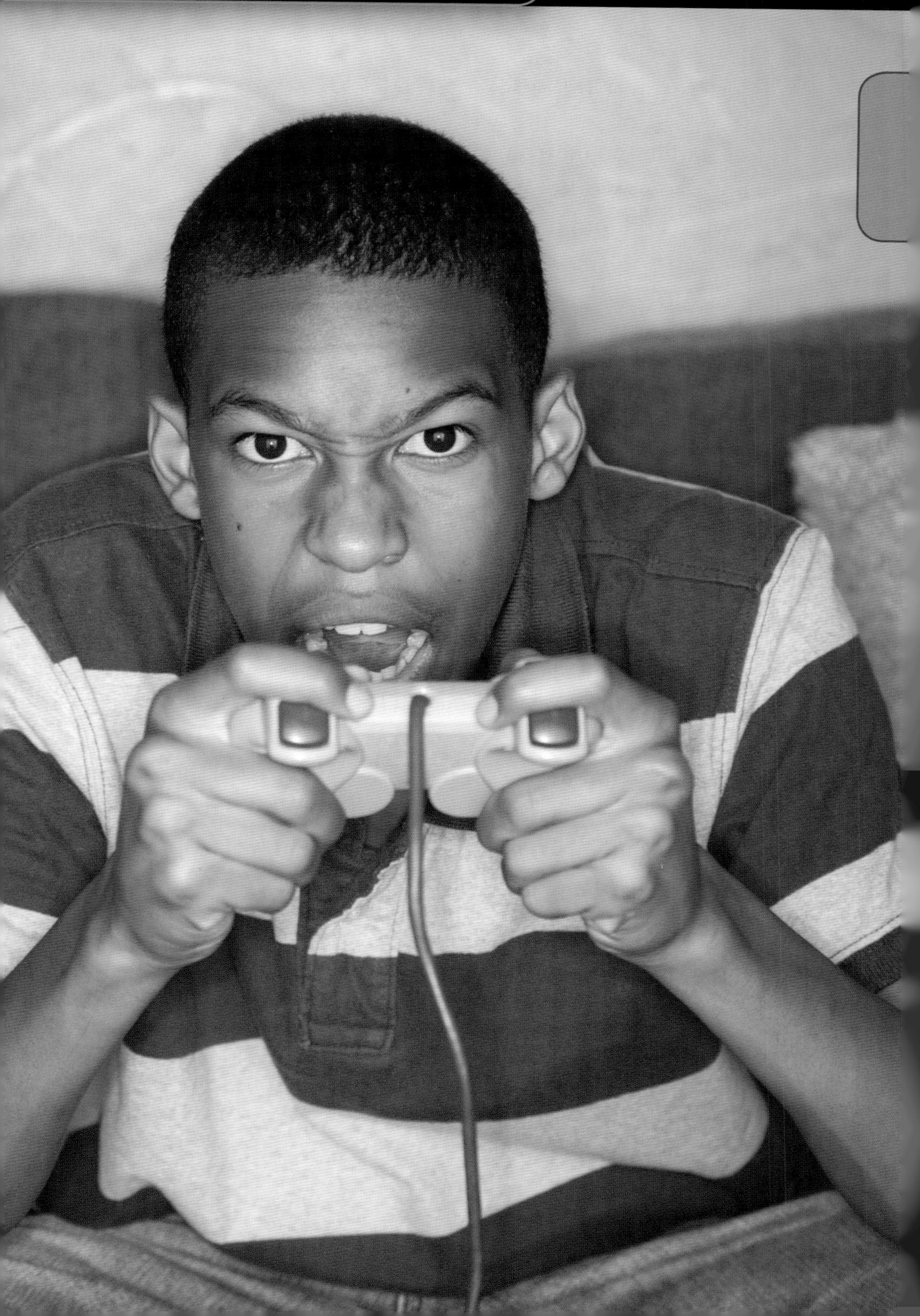

Violent video games and movies expose players and viewers to so much hateful, aggressive behavior that when violence occurs in real life, it lacks a "shock" effect.

children spend nearly fifty hours a week using electronic media, while spending only thirty hours per week in school and less than seventeen hours per week with their parents. The findings suggest that media plays an important influential role in childhood development.

TEN MOVIES ABOUT BULLYING

Hollywood has been addressing the issue of bullying for decades. Here's a list of some of the best known:

• **Carrie (1976).** This classic horror film was based on the novel by Stephen King. Carrie White is a shy high school girl whom her peers refuse to accept. They push her too far at the senior prom, and she terrorizes her small town.

• **Back to the Future (1985).** Marty goes thirty years back in time and changes history. The bully who harassed Marty's father into adulthood no longer wields power over him when Marty returns to the future.

• **Heathers (1988).** A clique of girls named Heather rule their high school. They are rich, pretty, and popular. But other kids are afraid of them—with good reason. They'll do anything—including murder—to "get" those they don't like.

(continued on the next page)

(continued from the previous page)

- ***Dazed and Confused* (1993).** On the last day of school, high school juniors and seniors haze or "initiate" kids who will be freshman in the fall. Boys endure physical assaults, and girls are verbally humiliated.

- ***Welcome to the Dollhouse* (1995).** Dawn Wiener is a junior high school student having a hard time. Peers regularly vandalize her locker, cheerleaders taunt her about her sexuality, and a boy named Brandon threatens her with sexual assault.

- ***Boys Don't Cry* (1999).** This true story of the rape and murder of a man who was transgender was the first mainstream movie about violence based on sexual orientation.

Hilary Swank and Chloë Sevigny star in the film *Boys Don't Cry*. The movie deals with sexual abuse and murder based on the victim's sexual orientation.

• **About a Boy (2002).** Marcus is a twelve-year-old who tries to please his mother by dressing in odd clothes and practicing vegetarianism. The kids at school reject him, and he tries to fit in. Later he decides to be himself and finds social support elsewhere.

• **Elephant (2003).** Roughly based on the 1999 shooting at Columbine High School, this film blames bullying and computer games for a high school massacre by two "outsiders" at a school dominated by athletes and beautiful people. (However, authorities have determined that bullying was not the reason for the actual shooting at Columbine.)

• **Mean Girls (2004).** Cady is the new girl at school. When she is bullied, she bullies others in return, creating an endless cycle of bullying and being bullied.

• **Toy Story 3 (2010).** A stuffed bear named Lotso menaces other toys in a day care center. Viewers ultimately learn that Lotso was abandoned as a young bear.

Peers, Neighborhoods, and Schools

Peer groups also influence whether bullying occurs and what happens if it does. In both schools and neighborhoods, peers often support or promote bullying behavior. Some kids who just want to fit in participate in bullying to feel part of the dominant group or avoid becoming targets themselves.

Most bullying happens in schools or during school-related activities. So the school culture affects how students and teachers perceive and act on bullying behavior. According to the National Association of School Psychologists (NASP), 25 percent of teachers see nothing wrong with bullying or putdowns. The NASP estimates that teachers intervene in only 4 percent of bullying incidents. If teachers ignore bullying behavior, they send the message that the behavior is OK. Ignoring it actually reinforces the bullying. But teacher intervention may not help the situation. If teachers give feedback, even if it's negative, they reward the bully with the attention he or she craves.

No matter what teachers and other school officials do, the fact is that more that two-thirds of students think adults in their school respond poorly to bullying, again according to

Most bullying takes place when no adults are around. Still, most targets think that teachers and other adults aren't much help even when they do see bullying behavior.

the NASP, and a majority of students say adult help is infrequent and ineffective.

WHY KIDS BULLY

Of course, blaming outside factors for bullying tells only part of the story. Well-known psychiatrist Dr. William Glasser proposed the idea that what a person wants at a given moment motivates all human behavior. He also said that nearly every human problem stems from feeling disconnected from others. Life experiences that threaten feelings of self-confidence, self-worth, self-determination, or connection with others contribute to negative actions toward others.

In the end, however, kids who bully choose to do so for one or more of seven major reasons:

1. They want power. With a goal of feeling important, kids bully to get the upper hand. They want to run things, get their way, or order others around.

2. They want to belong. Some kids bully because they feel unloved and disconnected. They desperately want to be accepted as part of a group. If the group bullies others, they will, too.

3. They want to have fun. Some kids actually enjoy seeing another person's pain. Others bully because making fun of someone makes them laugh.

4. They want freedom. Kids who feel little control over their lives bully to assert their ability to do whatever they want in a search for independence.

5. They want revenge or safety. Bullying sometimes happens in response to being bullied. Kids in this situation think they've been unfairly treated or wronged. They retaliate against the pain or injustice to make themselves feel safer. The retaliation may be directed at the person who bullied them or at someone they perceive as weaker.

6. They want to make up for feeling inferior. Kids who feel inadequate in some way bully to reduce the feeling or to feel superior to someone else.

7. They want attention. Some bullies need an audience. They'll take any kind of attention they can get. If they fail to get positive attention, they'll settle for the negative kind.

Kids who bully are simply trying to meet their perceived needs. Their actions seem to make sense to them at the time. However, choosing bullying behavior is not safe or healthy for anyone.

CHAPTER 4

WHY WON'T IT STOP?

According to the National Association of School Psychologists, bullying is the most common form of violence in our society. So it's easy to understand why, over time, kids who bully use violence to deal with their problems with little concern about possible consequences. Bullying affects everyone involved. Kids who bully, targets of bullies, and bystanders often share similar traits and results.

Kids who witness bullying—even if they don't participate in it—suffer negative effects. They experience guilt or helplessness if they don't stand up to a bully. Or they suffer emotional or physical harm if they do. They may rationalize the behavior and begin to think that bullying is acceptable.

Witnesses often have an increased use of tobacco, alcohol, or other drugs compared to peers, although this observation may result from hanging out with kids who bully—thus making it likely to see bullying incidents. Other bystanders suffer from depression, anxiety, and other mental

> Use—or abuse—of tobacco, alcohol, or other drugs has been associated with simply witnessing bullying behavior. Witnesses also experience mental health problems and outright fear even if they are not a target.

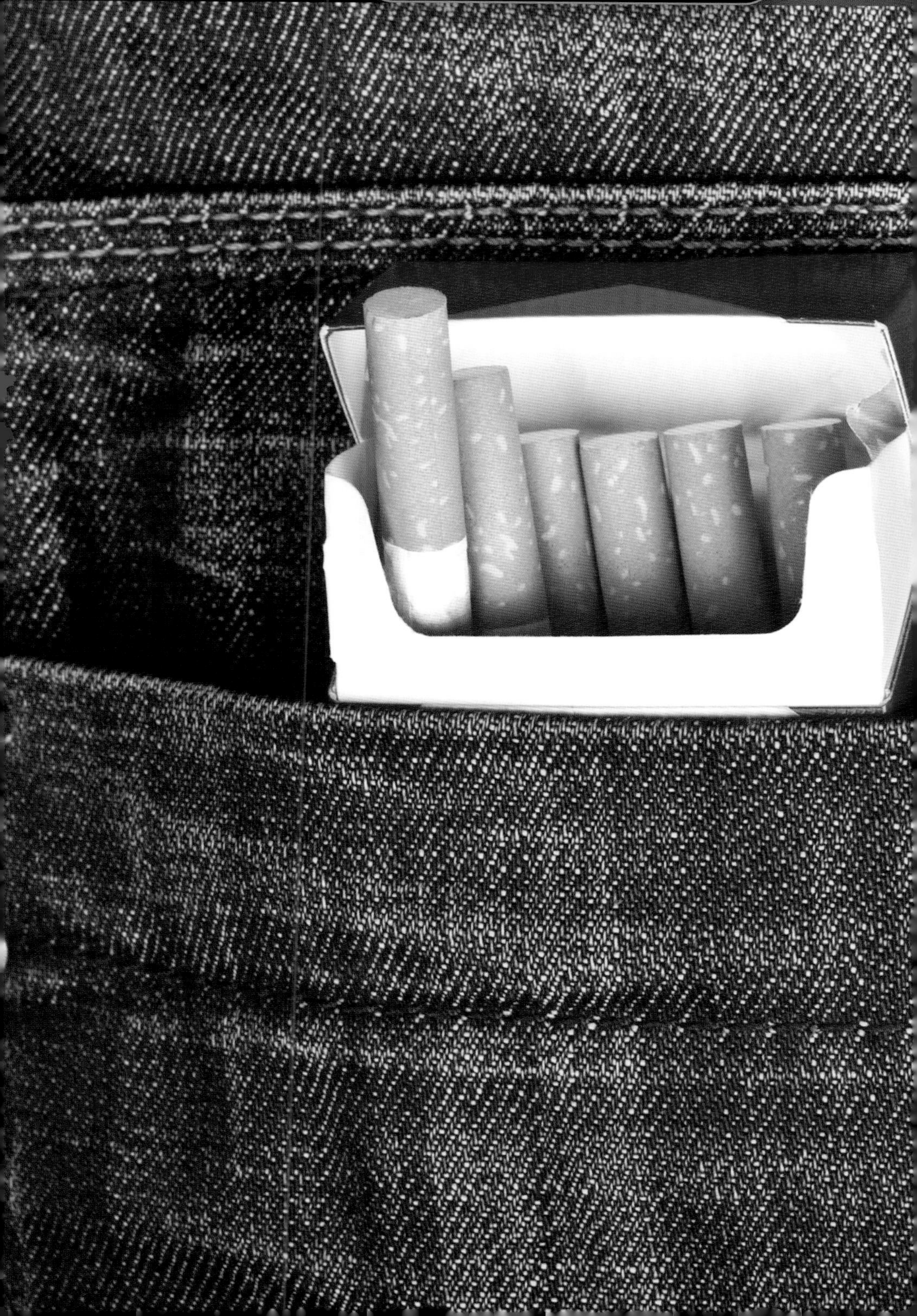

health problems. They can also experience outright fear. Some skip school because they don't feel safe there.

EFFECTS ON BULLIES

Compared to their peers, kids who bully more often abuse alcohol and other drugs than peers. They often participate in sexual activity at an earlier age. Bullies often suffer from low self-esteem, anxiety, or depression. And they're more likely than others to drop out of school.

Bullies get into more fights and violate more laws, committing acts from vandalism to serious crimes. They also have trouble with relationship skills and find it difficult to relate to peers and adults at school. Their classmates may seem to "respect" them, but the respect is borne of fear. Bullies are seldom well-liked.

Bullies have high hostility levels that have been shown to affect personal health. They may experience high blood pressure, changes in weight, unhealthy levels of blood fats called triglycerides, and insulin resistance, which makes it hard for the body to process sugar. High hostility levels corresponded with a high risk of heart disease and Type 2 diabetes.

Kids who participate in social bullying may be surprised when they lose friends and find it hard to make new ones. Other kids notice when the bully spreads gossip or false rumors about others. They realize that the bully might say the same kinds of things about them. Other kids also keep their distance and stop telling the bully their secrets, fearing that someday the secrets will be revealed to others.

Consequences to kids who bully continue into adulthood. They're more likely than peers to have criminal records and spend time in jail. They have trouble developing close friendships or romantic relationships. They can't form healthy relationships at work or home. And they're more likely to abuse spouses and children.

Effects on Targets

Kids who are bullied change both physically and emotionally. Over time, targets develop negative attitudes toward school, relationships, and society in general. If they try to ignore the bullying or react with fear, distress, or anxiety, the person who bullied them is encouraged to continue the behavior.

Targets often feel different, unpopular, powerless, misunderstood, and alone. They may lose whatever friends they had and come to feel like social outcasts. Targets develop insecurity, as well as low self-esteem and low self-confidence. These feelings get worse each time a new incident occurs.

Mental health professionals see a connection between being bullied and suffering from depression, marked by loss of interest in activities the target once enjoyed. A connection is also seen between being bullied and both sleep and eating disorders. These disorders may continue after the target reaches adulthood.

Headaches and stomachaches, along with more serious health issues such as diabetes and heart disease, affect many targets of bullying. Targets may also get involved with alcohol or other drugs.

The stress of dealing with bullying, as well as threats of future attacks, can cause such health issues as headaches, stomachaches, and trouble sleeping. The stress has been associated with less effective immune systems, so kids who are bullied often come down with actual illnesses. Like kids who bully, kids who are targeted often develop the same high hostility levels and share the same risks for heart disease and diabetes. Again, like their counterparts, targets may abuse alcohol and other drugs.

Targets are more likely than peers to have problems at school. In fact, according to SaveTeenRapp.org, an estimated 160,000 students skip school every day because they fear some form of bullying by other students. They miss or skip class and get lower grades and lower standardized test scores than peers do. They're less likely to participate in extracurricular activities where they could have found new friends and a sense of belonging. Many drop out of school altogether.

Kids who have been bullied sometimes retaliate against the bully or bully other kids. Targets may resort to violence when their pain and frustration become too much to handle. In a small number of cases, the violence is extreme. In some cases, young men who have committed fatal school shootings have a history of being bullied. However, in most cases, the bullying was only one of several contributing factors.

In alarming numbers, some targets turn the violence on themselves. They see no hope for escape and commit suicide. Fortunately, although targets of bullies are at risk of suicide, most don't even think about such behavior. Although sensational media reports often link bullying and self-destruction, other factors usually exist in addition to the abuse. A person who feels out of touch with peers or family may feel more so in the presence of a kid who bullies. By the same token, the effects of bullying on someone with a history of trauma or problems at home may be magnified.

INEFFECTIVE MEASURES

With all the negative outcomes associated with bullying behavior, it's hard to know why it continues. One reason might be that those trying to deal with it lack problem-solving skills. Targets, peers, and school personnel keep trying things that don't work.

For example, adults often tell kids who are bullied to ignore the behavior. However, a bully who fails to get a reaction of some kind from the target is likely to keep trying. The bullying becomes nastier and more frequent. The same goes for trying not to show tears or anger. The bully will still be motivated to escalate the situation.

WHY KIDS WHO ARE BULLIED DON'T TELL

Much bullying goes unreported. Those who suffer the pain and humiliation of bullying behavior often won't tell parents or teachers. Some major reasons for the silence include:

- They feel shame and think they did something to deserve it.

- They fear the person who bullied them will get them back.

- They think telling will do no good—that no one will help them.

- They think the bully is so strong that no one can help them.

- They don't trust adults because adults in their lives also behave like bullies.

- They think telling shows immaturity—that "big" kids are supposed to "take it" without whining or "crying home to Mama."

- They fear losing phone or Internet privileges at home.

Experts agree that targets should refrain from engaging in the same bullying behavior as their tormenters. Calling names, shouting insults, or making threats turns a victim into a perpetrator. So does physically fighting back—even in self-defense. Above all, nothing good can come from turning around and bullying someone else.

Responding to cyberbullying potentially creates more trouble. Replying creates the temptation to answer in kind—thus turning a bad situation worse. As with in-person bullying, the cyberbully wants a reaction from the target. Giving one to him or her only serves to encourage the behavior.

Responding to online bullying by lashing out or showing that you're upset rewards the bully with the attention he or she seeks and encourages more of the bad behavior.

WHAT PEERS DO WRONG

Kids and teens who witness bullying may want to make it stop but not know what to do. They stand and watch, which rewards the bully with an audience. They remain silent, fearing that telling an adult what's going on will make them a "snitch." Or they think the affair is none of their business and refrain from getting involved—even when someone's personal safety is at risk. Some stop associating with the target to keep from lowering their own social status or becoming targets themselves.

Other kids and teens react to bullying by letting themselves be drawn into the situation by group pressure. They join in the "fun." They may not start the lies, rumors, gossip, and other hurtful messages about

RISKY CYBER BUSINESS

Anyone can be a target for a cyberbully, but you don't have to make it easy. Avoid or limit these Internet practices to minimize your risk:

- Using Facebook, Twitter, or similar sites

- Talking with strangers in chat rooms

- Accepting instant messages from unknown sources

- Putting personal information, phone numbers, addresses, or pictures online

- Adding a guestbook to a website

- Adding a comments feature to a blog

- Using a password that someone could easily guess (phone number, birth date, address, etc.)

- Giving out e-mail or social network passwords

- Using a password hint (for remembering a password) that others can figure out

- Sending nude or embarrassing images online

- Participating in online games

someone, but they spread them to others, including forwarding cyberbullying messages.

CAMPUS COPS

Teachers and other personnel may indeed mean well, but they have traditionally failed to curb bullying behavior in schools. Some ignore it, thinking the kids will work it out themselves.

Others play the role of private investigator. They try to sort out the facts right away. They question participants at the scene of the event. They force bystanders to tell what they saw—in front of other people. Or they talk to the kid

School officials have tried to curb bullying by using zero-tolerance policies and hiring security personnel. However, these efforts have failed to stop bullies.

who bullied and the kid who was bullied together instead of speaking privately to each party.

In their defense, school officials have tried a number of other measures to combat bullying behavior. They have installed metal detectors and surveillance cameras. They've hired security personnel to patrol the halls and grounds. They've enacted zero-tolerance policies and suspended or expelled offenders. Unfortunately, experience shows that none of these efforts works.

CHAPTER 5

COPING WITH BULLYING

Nadin Khoury hated to hear the dismissal bell at the end of the school day. The thirteen-year-old, smaller-than-average kid knew he was going to get beat up. It happened every day on the way home. The daily attacks started at the beginning of the school year with name-calling by a group of boys. The boys also made fun of Nadin's mother for her Liberian citizenship.

On January 11, 2011, though, the abuse took a different turn. In a thirty-minute-long attack, six boys ages thirteen to seventeen punched him, kicked him, dragged him through the snow, stuffed him upside down in a tree, and stuck him on a tall fence by his jacket. A seventh boy recorded the assault on his mobile phone as Nadin screamed for them to stop. The photographer later posted the footage on YouTube.

"I was scared and angry," he later said, quoted in the *New York Daily News*. "All you can do is sit there and wait for it to be over."

Nadin's mother encouraged the boy to go to the police. In a supreme act of courage, he did just that. The police entered Upper Darby High School in the Philadelphia suburb of Drexel, Pennsylvania, and handcuffed six of the alleged attackers. The seventh suspect was arrested the next day.

Such bullying as destruction of property, theft, physical attack, threats of harm, and some cyber attacks are crimes. Contact law enforcement. If a threat is imminent, call 911. Electronic sexually suggestive or naked images of anyone younger than eighteen qualify as child pornography. Call your local police or the Federal Bureau of Investigation (FBI). Bullying based on race, color, national origin, sex, disability, or religion violates the Civil Rights Act. Contact the U.S. Department of Justice Office for Civil Rights.

Most important, keep looking for help. You might find a few trusted peers you can enlist to help you. Keep reporting the abuse to adults. If your efforts to get them to listen seem to fail, don't give up. Continue to report the abuse—even if you must report it to different adults.

IT'S A CRIME

Police charged them with kidnapping, aggravated assault, criminal restraint, terroristic threats, reckless endangering of another person, and conspiracy. One of the boys, age fourteen, had two previous assault charges. After court, all but one of the boys served time until the end of the school year. The last boy was sent for drug treatment. Nadin changed to a new school where he felt safe.

Nadin was far from a lone victim of physical bullying in the United States. According to SaveTeenRapp. org, 46 percent of males and 26 percent of females say they have been physically attacked. To let them all know they aren't alone, Nadin and his mother appeared on the ABC talk show *The View* to tell his story.

During the interview, his favorite National Football League (NFL) player, Philadelphia Eagles wide receiver

DeSean Jackson, along with two Eagles linemen, surprised him. Jackson understood Nadin's plight. As a child, the Pro Bowler was smaller than other kids and often found himself the target of bullies.

Jackson applauded Nadin's bravery for standing up. "I promise any time you ever need us—if anything like this keeps happening again—I got two linemen right here. Let us know," he said. "We got you."

STANDING UP

Not every kid who gets bullied has an NFL team watching his or her back. But if you are on the receiving end of bullying behavior, you can take steps to minimize the effects. Kids who bully count on little or no resistance from their targets. In some cases, simply telling a bully to "stop" or "leave me alone" puts an end to

Fake it 'til you make it. Bullies will look elsewhere for a target if you act confident and unafraid (even if you don't feel that way).

the behavior. Sometimes you can simply walk away from the situation. If not, yell for help.

Body language can also discourage a bully. Avoid slouching or looking down when a bully confronts you. Stand up straight and look the person in the eye. Act confident—even if you don't feel that way. A bully wants to make you look weak. If you give off the image of strength, the bully usually looks elsewhere for a weaker target.

Take preventive steps. Avoid being alone, especially in restrooms and lunch halls. Look for new ways to get to and from school to steer clear of routes the bullies take. In the school building, use different hallways to reach your classrooms. Try to walk with a group. There is often safety in numbers. Seek out a few kids you can trust. Explain what is happening and how it affects you. Ask for their support.

HOTLINES AND HELPLINES

Several organizations provide free and confidential hotlines and helplines for kids who are bullied or considering suicide. Website URLs and phone numbers can change. If you don't get through, don't give up. Use an Internet search engine to find these groups.

Boys Town National Hotline

You can talk with professional counselors by phone or online any time day or night all year. This hotline is accredited by the American Association of Suicidiology.
(http://www.yourlifeyourvoice.org)
(800) 448-3000

Kids Help Phone (Canada)

(800) 668-6868
This twenty-four-hour Canadian helpline provides professional counselors and referrals in both French and English. The website offers information about all types of bullying.
(http://www.kidshelpphone.ca)

National Suicide Prevention Lifeline

(800) 273-8255
If you're thinking about suicide, you can reach a caring counselor who wants to help. You'll talk to a trained counselor in your area.
(http://www.suicidepreventionlifeline.org)

National Teen Dating Abuse Helpline

(866) 331-9474
Originally called "Love Is Respect," this helpline is designed specifically for teens and young adults. It offers real-time, one-on-one support from trained peer advocates through phone, text, and chat services.

Stomp Out Bullying Help Line
(855) 790-4357
Counselors at this live chat line are trained to help kids older than thirteen who are being bullied. (http://www.stompoutbullying.org/livechat_portal.php)

If the bullying happens at school, report it to a teacher, school counselor, or principal. However, don't be surprised if school officials do little to help. Although bullying awareness and prevention programs are aimed at educators, some of them are still learning how to respond to student-to-student abuse. If you don't get help in your school, go to the district superintendent or the state department of education.

CUTTING DOWN THE NET

If someone uses electronic media to abuse you, keep evidence of the attacks. Record the dates and times they occur. And write down a description of what happened. Print out screenshots, e-mails, and texts and save them. Block everyone who sends them. Forward offensive text messages to a trusted adult, and ask for help. Resist the temptation to respond.

Some cyberbullies try to remain anonymous. However, you can often figure out who they are. Pay attention to the words a bully uses. Kids who bully online often use the same words they use in person. Sometimes they refer to actual events they participated in. Or they talk about something that happened in a particular class or sports practice. Those clues can help you narrow down who belongs to the anonymous cyber voice. A tech-savvy friend or adult may be able to get a website operator to trace the Internet Protocol (IP) address of the sender and identify who owns the screen name.

Open messages only from people you know. Instead, leave messages from strangers unopened. If the communication persists, change your e-mail address, account, username, and password on all electronic communications. Always protect your contact information. Make it hard for someone to learn your e-mail or home address, phone number, instant-messaging screen name, or website URL. Use a code name for your e-mail address and screen name. Keep your passwords secret (that's what they're for). To control who sees your account, adjust your privacy settings on social networking sites.

Don't give cyberbullies ammunition. Never post pictures or private information that you wouldn't want to see broadcasted on a network news channel. And never give out personal information such as your age or the name of your school.

Look for support groups for kids who are bullied. You may find them in your community, as well as online. Knowing you're not alone may offer some comfort. A group may also give you advice about how to handle your situation. If your school has no anti-bullying group, ask the principal to start one.

Join new activities. Take a karate or self-defense class. Learn to relax by trying yoga. You might even

Self-defense classes help develop self-confidence in kids who are the targets of bullies. Techniques learned can also help targets defend themselves against physical bullying.

meet new friends who make you feel accepted. Some kids find relief by writing in a journal. Or you might write a letter to the bully explaining your feelings. You don't have to deliver the letter; just writing it may help. Another writing exercise is to write a list of the positive things in your life. This will help you think about those instead of constantly worrying about the kid who is bullying you.

Feeling overwhelmed, anxious, or depressed is a normal reaction to bullying. Although some kids who are bullied contemplate or even commit suicide, you don't have to be one of them. Visit trusted websites, blogs, or such hotlines as the National Suicide Prevention Lifeline. Or seek help from a school counselor, social worker, or mental health professional.

Cyberbullying violates terms of service established by many Internet service providers, social media sites, and mobile phone services. Report the bullying to them.

Some online actions warrant more drastic measures. If someone posts untrue information that negatively affects your reputation or posts something that invades your privacy (even if it's true), you may have grounds for a civil lawsuit for monetary damages. Ask your parents to contact an attorney.

CHAPTER 6

When a new ninth-grade boy wore a pink shirt on his first day at Central Kings Rural High School in Cambridge, Nova Scotia, Canada, in 2007, a group of boys taunted him. They called him a homosexual for wearing pink and threatened to beat him up.

Two other boys weren't having any of it. Seniors David Shepherd and Travis Price mounted an online "Sea of Pink" campaign. They bought fifty pink tank tops at a discount store and e-mailed fellow students asking them to wear the shirts the next day to support the hapless freshman.

The next day David and Travis handed out the shirts as their classmates arrived. Some kids wore the shirts the seniors bought. Others wore their own pink clothes. A few even dressed in pink head-to-toe. By the time the new kid got there, a sea of pink greeted him.

"Definitely it looked like there was a big weight lifted off his shoulders," David said in a CBC News story. "He went from looking right depressed to being as happy as can be."

The bullies were nowhere to be seen.

David credited "a little activism" for the outcome. "If you can get more people against [bullies]… to show that we're not going to put up with it and support each other, then they're not as big a group as they think are," he told the CBC.

Pink Shirt Day is celebrated on the last Wednesday in February in schools across Canada to take a stand against bullying. This photo was taken at Point Grey Secondary School in Vancouver, British Columbia, in 2013.

"Finally, someone stood up for a weaker kid," Travis told CKNW News Talk, an AM radio station in Vancouver, British Columbia, thousands of miles across Canada. The movement caught on throughout Canada and the United States, with annual Pink Shirt Day celebrations. In 2013, more than 160,000 people used Facebook to commit to wearing pink and helping stop bullying, according to CKNW radio.

NICE IT FORWARD

Another student-led initiative is the Nice It Forward movement started by Kevin Curwick that uses social media to put an end to bullying. The high school football player in Osseo, Minnesota, near Minneapolis, started a Twitter account to tweet nice things about his classmates.

The messages reported by author Justin Patchin on his blog included such statements as:

- "The nicest girl ever"
- "Always has his heart in the right place"
- "The best break dancer"

Soon other students in the Minneapolis-St. Paul area started their own Twitter accounts to fight bullying. They, too, tweeted positive messages about their schools and other students.

The idea caught on around the United States, and many more Nice It Forward Twitter accounts were born. The teens involved stepped up on their own—without a nudge or help from adults—to show that bullying is not acceptable. The movement also helps kids who are bullied realize that they are not alone. Their peers support them.

WHAT ONE PERSON CAN DO

You don't have to start a nationwide anti-bullying campaign to help minimize or stop bullying and its effects. You can first set a good example by refusing to participate either as a bully, tagalong, or a "none of my business" bystander.

Learn to recognize abusive behavior when you see it. Be a friend to the target. Comfort him or her the best you can. Even if you think you risk becoming the next target or

Simply comforting a peer who is bullied shows the target that she or he is not alone. Telling a bully to stop is another way to support victims.

being excluded from the "cool" group, speak up. Tell the bully to stop. According to Kimberly L. Mason, Ph.D., in *Bullying No More*, studies show that in 57 percent of cases where a bystander intervenes in a bullying situation, the bullying usually stops within ten seconds.

REPORTING OR TATTLING?

Some kids who witness bullying won't tell an adult because they don't want to "tattle" on fellow students. But tattling on someone and reporting abusive behavior that puts someone's emotional or physical safety at risk are not the same things.

It's easy to tell the difference: The goal of tattling is to get someone in trouble. The goal of reporting is to help remove someone from potential danger.

The rule applies not only to acts of bullying behavior, but also to reactions to it.

For example, a kid who is bullied may display a change in mood or behavior. Showing signs of depression, giving away possessions, or saying strange good-byes to others may precede a suicide attempt. Reporting these types of observations is aimed at helping the person, not getting him or her in trouble.

If you notice someone who seems sad or anxious or is having trouble getting things done or taking care of himself or herself, bullies may be to blame. Turn to a school official or tell your parents. Ask them to contact the school and the target's parents.

Another way to help is to report rumors of such planned bullying activity as a fight after school. Alerting authorities can prevent harm before it happens.

If the target is surrounded by a group of bullies, look for a way to help him or her escape. Create a distraction or help the target get away. Grab the target by the hand and say "Come with me" or "We need to go" and walk away together. However, in a case of physical bullying, avoid stepping in if you risk physical harm. Instead, quickly find an adult to help.

If no adults are present or willing to help, look for another adult who is. Reporting abuse is always important. For help in knowing what to do, visit trusted websites that offer suggestions of ways to combat bullying. Or start an anti-bullying program in your school. Some schools have peer mediation systems on playgrounds or after school. Such systems send the message: we don't tolerate bullying. If your school doesn't have one, start one.

WORKING TOGETHER

You can help others get involved. Participate in Pink Shirt Day awareness campaigns or start your own Nice It Forward Twitter account. Recruit other kids to work as a team to condemn bullying behavior—both in general and in specific cases. Surprisingly, even a small group of defenders can make a big difference. If the bullying doesn't stop altogether, the person who is being bullied will at least know he or she has support and doesn't have to face the abuse alone. If you notice situations or locations in the school building where bullying is prevalent, tell school officials when and where more adult supervision is needed.

Ask if the school has an anti-bullying policy. If so, ask to see a copy and review it. Does it cover the activities you see around school? Do you see ways to improve the policy? Make a list of suggestions and discuss it with

the principal or another school official. If your school does not have an anti-bullying program, ask to start one.

You might start a school club to fight bullying. Come up with ideas that encourage increased respect among peers. Plan activities to condemn bullying behavior. For instance, club members could start a letter-writing campaign to the school newspaper or local print and broadcast media to build awareness. The club could make and display anti-bullying posters or create public service announcements to be read with the school's morning announcements. Or the members could make a video and post it on YouTube, Facebook, or other social media.

Amanda Tyson, an Oregon student who was bullied from middle school through college, started a "Be Kind" anti-bullying Facebook page. In 2014, the page showed sixty-six thousand likes.

You can start a schoolwide pledge campaign through a club or just with an informal group of friends. Order T-shirts, buttons, pins, or magnets to give out when someone pledges to stamp out bullying by refusing to participate in it and promising to speak up when it occurs.

TEXAS TEEN WINS "UNITE AGAINST BULLYING COMMERCIAL CHALLENGE"

With a two-minute video titled "Word Play," Lauren Bush, an eighth grader at St. John's Episcopal School in Dallas, Texas, won the 2014 "Unite Against Bullying Commercial Challenge."

Middle school and high school students submitted anti-bullying essays and videos with ideas for a public service announcement, an advertisement in the public interest aired at no charge. Lauren's film showed the power of words in bullying situations. In the film, a girl who has been bullied changes her attitude as fellow students label her with such positive words as fun, smart, and beautiful to replace such negative labels as dumb, loser, and ugly.

Lauren won a trip to Los Angeles, California, to see her idea professionally filmed. The PSA later aired on the USA Network and YouTube. The winner also appeared on NBC's *Today* news show and said she hoped to inspire others and show that it only takes one person to take a stand against bullying.

She and two other runners-up also won an iPad. The USA Network, together with Characters Unite and R&R Partners Foundation's Flip the Script anti-bullying campaign, sponsored the contest.

You can view the video on YouTube.

MORE ANTI-BULLYING ACTIVITIES

Learn all you can about bullying's causes and effects. Articles, books, blogs, and websites offer extensive information on the topic. You can also develop your own online resources for your friends. Create your own blog, website, or Facebook group to discuss the issue. Link to other helpful sites.

Learn how to use phones, tablets, computers, and all electronic media responsibly. List ways to stay safe from cyberbullying. Share the information with friends. Look at each other's posts on social media and discuss ways to keep them appropriate. Delete all personal information that could lead an unknown person to your school or home. And encourage friends not to participate in passing along mean messages they may receive about others.

Finally, mentor younger kids. You can do this one-on-one or work together with teachers to develop an online safety program to present in lower grades. Share your own experiences and teach younger users how to avoid trouble and what to do if they become a target of cyberbullies.

10 Great Questions to Ask a School Counselor

1. How can I notify an Internet Service Provider (ISP) if someone breaks a website's rules about bad language, inappropriate comments, or threats?

2. Does our school have a bullying prevention program?

3. Where can I find a mental health professional to help me deal with the anxiety and depression from being bullied?

4. Which helplines or chat lines can I trust?

5. What do I do if I want to change schools to get away from kids who bully?

6. My boyfriend or girlfriend wants me to text him or her naked pictures of myself. What should I do?

7. Are there any community resources that deal with bullying prevention?

8. Where can I find a support group for kids who are bullied?

9. I got an anonymous note threatening to kill me. What should I do?

10. How can I protect younger students from kids who beat them up after school?

CHAPTER 7

Putting an end to all types of bullying requires the participation and commitment of educators, parents, and members of the community. Significant changes in attitudes are needed to transform the climate where kids grow up. The new dynamic dispels the ideas that bullying is a necessary part of growing up, that it should be ignored, and that nothing can be done about it.

Schools should focus on prevention rather than waiting to react to incidents when they occur. Administrators must create a positive school environment that includes rules of conduct and fair, consistent disciplinary measures.

The school's role should begin as early as possible. Even toddlers in preschool can learn positive attitudes and appropriate ways to deal with conflicts and interact with others. As they enter elementary school, they should get social skills training in programs selected and presented by school psychologists or mental health professionals. These professionals should also intervene when aggressive behavior occurs and provide counseling when needed.

A good school-centered, anti-bullying program should involve the entire school, including teachers and students. It should also include teacher and parent training. Teachers

Even preschool toddlers can learn ways to deal with conflict and frustration without physical, emotional, or verbal abuse. Learning to use positive attitudes is a good first step in bullying prevention.

need training in how to identify bullying and what to do in response. They also need to know how to model correct behavior and give positive feedback for appropriate actions.

Parents need to learn how to recognize bullies and their targets and how to spot behavior patterns suggesting that their children are being bullied—or are the aggressors. With support from such school professionals as psychologists, social workers, and counselors, parents can learn to show children how to interact with others by example.

Elements of a Good School-Based Anti-Bullying Program

A schoolwide anti-bullying campaign has the best chance for success if it incorporates the following key elements:

- Participation by students, teachers, administrators, and parents
- Ways to identify bullying
- How to step in safely

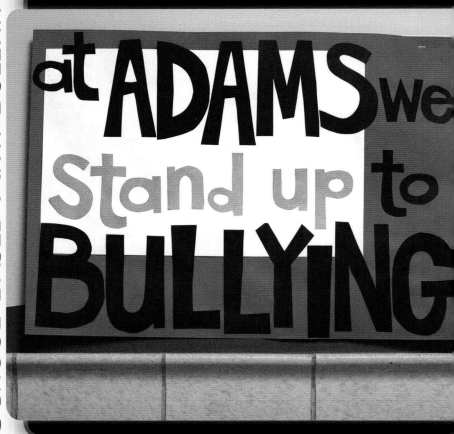

A schoolwide anti-bullying campaign at Adams Elementary School in Janesville, Wisconsin, aims at reducing negative behavior among students.

- Where to report bullying
- Classroom discussions about supporting targets
- Consistent application and management of anti-bullying policies
- Effective discipline for bad behavior

WHAT PARENTS CAN DO

Even the best school-centered, anti-bullying programs will not have good results without support from students' parents. Parents must know what kinds of help are available from school personnel and how to get that help. Parents must also become aware of discipline policies and support them. When a bullying situation arises, parents of both the child who bullies and the target should immediately contact school officials and work together to help both students. Parents of kids who bully should know and teach their children why their behavior is wrong.

For parents, as well as school personnel, the focus should be on prevention. Start early to show how to resolve conflicts without aggression, and give kids positive feedback when their actions reflect care and concern for others. At home, parents should avoid physical punishment for misbehavior and instead take away privileges in response.

Even though most of today's parents know a lot less about technology than their children do, learning the ins

Parents' involvement is important in curbing bullying behavior. Schoolwide campaigns should include instruction for parents so that they can teach their children appropriate ways to handle conflict.

and outs of Internet use is vital. Parents need to establish rules about and monitor their kids' use of cell phones and other electronic media. The rules should include what kids can do online and which sites they can visit.

Parents should prohibit kids from using technology to share private or embarrassing information about themselves or others. Parents should also teach children how to stay safe online. Finally, parents should encourage their kids to tell them immediately if they—or their friends— become targets of cyberbullies.

COMMUNITY EFFORTS

If the saying "It takes a village to raise a child" is correct, it follows that it takes a village to protect youth from bullying. Bullying affects society as a whole, so community involvement is important. Educators who develop anti-bullying policies are working to combat the behavior. So are government representatives who enact anti-bullying ordinances and laws. So are many community organizations.

No federal law specifically outlaws bullying. In 2011, in response to a teen suicide associated with bullying based on sexual orientation, the Safe Schools Improvement

Home | StopBullying.gov

www.stopbullying.gov

Home | StopBullying.gov

What You Can Do | Blog | Newsroom | Images | Videos | Resour

stopbullying.gov

| WHAT IS BULLYING | CYBER BULLYING | WHO IS AT RISK | PREVENT BULLYING | RESPOND BULLYING |

FEATURES

LGBT Pride Month

Labels Video

▸ Be More Than a Bystander

Laws and Policies

Get a new perspective on bullying.

Take a walk in your kid's shoes and learn how they can safely stop bullying.

WHAT YOU CAN DO

Parents

Educators

Community

Teens

UPDATES

STATE POLICIE

StopBullying.gov is a federal government website managed by U.S. Department of Health and Human Services. It offers resour for students, parents, teachers, and communities to help iden prevent, and respond to bullying behavior.

Act was introduced in the U.S. Senate. Senator Bob Casey, a Democrat from Pennsylvania, and Senator Mark Kirk, a Republican from Illinois, introduced the bill, which would have added bullying prevention programs to the Safe and Drug-Free Schools and Communities Act. Also in 2011, Senator Al Franken of Minnesota and congressman Jared Polis of Colorado, both Democrats, introduced the Student Non-Discrimination Act, which would have added sexual orientation and gender identity to federal education nondiscrimination law. Both bills died in committee.

However, bullying based on race, color, national origin, gender, disability, or religion is often covered by laws banning harassment. These types of incidents may be reported to the U.S. Department of Education's Office for Civil Rights or the U.S. Department of Justice's Civil Rights Division.

State laws and policies that address bullying do exist in all fifty states. In 1999, Georgia was the first state to enact a law against bullying and violence among students. The Georgia codes cover character education, bullying, student codes of conduct, safety rules on school buses, disciplinary policies, and penalties for disrupting public schools.

According to StopBullying.gov, Montana is the only state with no anti-bullying laws, but it does have a state model policy that schools can use as a basis for their own policies. Arizona, Illinois, Indiana, Kansas, Minnesota, North Dakota,

Singer Carly Rae Jepsen was one of the performers at the 2013 #UniteLIVE: The Concert to Rock Out Bullying in Las Vegas, Nevada. The concert was an example of community activities aimed at wiping out bullying.

Tennessee, and Texas have such laws in effect. The rest of the states have both laws and model school policies.

COMMUNITY ACTIVITIES

Many community activities help raise awareness of the toll that intolerance and aggressive behavior take on society at large. For example, on October 3, 2012, the Thomas & Mack Center at the University of Nevada, Las Vegas, was the site of #UniteLIVE: The Concert to Rock Out Bullying. The event featured Carly Rae Jepsen, Nolan Gould, Sheamus, James Roday, and Mehcad Brooks.

TIPS FOR COMMUNITIES

Parent Further, a search institute resource for families, has created tips for community members who want to get involved in addressing bullying issues. They include the following ideas:

• Provide mentoring opportunities for young people in your neighborhood or through such organizations as Big Brothers Big Sisters of America.

• Offer youth opportunities to volunteer at neighborhood or community events, serve on committees, or assist at hospitals, libraries, food pantries, or other places that need help.

• Be a good neighbor. Develop a relationship with kids who live around you. Show interest in their activities.

• Set a good example by communicating well and resolving adult conflicts in nonviolent ways.

• Create cross-cultural experiences for youth in the community.

• Work to promote a safe place to play, and do your part to watch out for the neighborhood kids.

• Promote positive values by behaving with integrity, responsibility, and restraint yourself.

• Create ways youth can investigate future careers with job shadowing, career fairs, and internships.

Thousands of middle and high school students, parents, and educators from the Las Vegas area turned out to commemorate National Bullying Prevention Month. Sponsors hoped it was the first step toward reaching hundreds of thousands more young people with their message of respect and acceptance of others. Concert sponsors included the USA Network's Characters Unite, R&R Partners Foundation's anti-bullying youth project Flip the Script, and Cox Communications.

Characters Unite also sponsors the "I Won't Stand for It" movement that lets participants send messages to fight hate and intolerance. It's a public service campaign that features musicians, actors, athletes, politicians, and others who refuse to stand by in the face of racism, bullying, religious intolerance, and other forms of discrimination. Participants are encouraged to visit the Characters Unite website and post their own photos and thoughts. The campaign has reached more than twenty-seven million people.

Another campaign called NFL Characters Unite lets professional football players share their stories in an effort to reach youth who have issues with prejudice, bullying, or discrimination. Featured players have included Green Bay Packers wide receiver Randall Cobb, New York Jets center Nick Mangold, Baltimore Ravens running back Ray Rice, Chicago Bears cornerback Charles Tillman, Houston Texans defensive end J. J. Watt, and wide receiver Victor Cruz and linebacker Mark Herzlich of the New York Giants.

BULLY-FREE SUMMER CAMPS

When school is out for summer, some kids leave the campus and head to another environment where bullying may run rampant. Some kids' summer day camp or sleepover camp experiences were so horrible that the bad feelings stay with them into adulthood.

Just like bullying that occurs in schools, bullying at summer camps most often occurs out of sight of counselors or other adults—during free time, en route to activities, in shower rooms, or in the bunkhouse after lights out. Fortunately, many camp administrators have been made aware of the risk of intolerance and aggressive behavior at their sites.

The American Camp Association (ACA) has taken steps to create camping environments free from bullying. It provides a sample camp policy that can be personalized for its nine thousand professional members to use at their camps. The ACA also supplies tip sheets for staff training and a sample letter to inform parents about a camp's anti-bullying policies. Some camps also include camper training the first day of camp to prevent unwanted behavior during the session and to encourage campers to report bullying.

The ACA advises parents to ask about their children's camp's policies and to inform them ahead of time

Mark Herzlich Jr., linebacker for the New York Giants of the National Football League (NFL), shared his own story about bullying at the third annual NFL Characters Unite event in 2014 in New York.

if a child has been bullied in the past. Preparing children for camp should include discussions about how to react if someone tries to bully them and what to do if they feel unsafe at any time during the session.

Community involvement is a key ingredient in stamping out aggression and violence. Awareness is increasing. And—finally—there is hope that kids who bully and those who are bullied will soon find new ways to deal with conflict so that bullying is no longer accepted as a normal part of growing up.

GLOSSARY

bigotry Intolerance of people who fall outside one's own group based on race, religion, politics, or other factors.

bullying Unwanted, aggressive behavior with a goal of harming or controlling another person.

clique A small group of people who share the same interests and who spend time together, excluding others.

cyberbullying Bullying that takes place using the Internet.

fetal alcohol syndrome A condition in a child whose mother abused alcohol during pregnancy. Effects include physical deformity, mental or learning disabilities, and behavioral problems.

gender stereotype A standardized, oversimplified concept of how males and females should dress or act.

hazing A type of bullying used to initiate a new person into a group.

indirect bullying Attacks made by another person on behalf of the bully; also called proxy bullying.

Internet Protocol (IP) address A binary number that identifies and locates every individual computer and other electronic device.

physical bullying Bullying that involves touching another person or the person's property in a mean way intended to intimidate or humiliate the target.

proxy A person who acts in another's place; a substitute or representative.

sexting Sending nude, suggestive, or sexually explicit images or messages via a cell phone or mobile device.

taunting Mocking, often done by a bully to insult or humiliate a target.

teasing Light-hearted fun among friends with no intent to hurt.

verbal bullying Bullying that involves words, either spoken or written.

FOR MORE INFORMATION

American Association of Suicidology (AAS)
5221 Wisconsin Avenue NW
Washington, DC 20015
(202) 237-2280
Website: http://www.suicidology.org

Members of AAS are people touched by suicide or who are involved in suicide prevention and intervention. The organization promotes research, education, and training. It also develops resources and support services for suicide survivors.

Anti-Defamation League (ADL)
605 Third Avenue
New York, NY, 10158
(212) 885-7700
Website: http://adl.org

The Anti-Defamation League was founded to fight anti-Semitism and other forms of bigotry in the United States and overseas. It develops materials, programs, and services to build understanding and respect among diverse groups.

Born This Way Foundation, Inc.
10736 Jefferson Boulevard #525
Culver City, CA 90230
Website: http://bornthiswayfoundation.org

Lady Gaga and her mother, Cynthia Germanotta, founded the Born This Way Foundation in 2011 to encourage a social atmosphere that embraces differences and celebrates individuality. The foundation works to help all people, but it often is associated with those who are bullied because of their sexual orientation.

Boys Town

14100 Crawford Street
Boys Town, NE 68010
(402) 498-1300
Website: http://www.boystown.org

Boys Town's mission is to save children and heal families. Its work for both boys and girls includes reuniting kids with their families, finding foster homes for others, and providing a Boys Town family for those with nowhere else to turn. It operates a national bilingual hotline with professional counselors who speak English and Spanish, as well as those who use Telecommunications Device for the Deaf (TDD) lines for callers who are deaf or have speech impairments.

BullyingCanada

471 Smythe Street
P.O. Box 27009
Fredericton, NB E3B 9M1
Canada
(877) 352-4497
E-mail: support@bullyingcanada.ca
Website: http://bullyingcanada.ca

This all-volunteer organization operates a website created by Canadian youth. It offers information about bullying, a video library, a newsletter, and resource contacts.

Canadian Association for Suicide Prevention (CASP)

870 Portage Avenue
Winnipeg, MB R3G 0P1
Canada
(204) 784-4073

E-mail: casp@suicideprevention.ca
Website: http://www.suicideprevention.ca

The Canadian Association for Suicide Prevention is an organization of professionals that provides information and resources aimed at reducing the suicide rate.

Champions Against Bullying

650 Poydras Street, Suite 1470
New Orleans, LA 70131
E-mail: info@championsagainstbullying.com
Website: http://www.championsagainstbullying.com

Champions Against Bullying is a nonprofit organization that works to give school children the chance to learn in an environment free from fear, violence, and limitations.

Gay, Lesbian & Straight Education Network (GLSEN)

90 Broad St.
New York, NY 10004
(212) 727-0135
E-mail: glsen.org
Website: http://www.glsen.org/

Founded in 1990 by a group of Massachusetts teachers, GLSEN is a national education organization that helps created a school environment where lesbian, gay, bisexual, and transgender students can learn and grow free from bullying.

Not in Our School

P.O. Box 70232
Oakland, CA 94612
(510) 268-9675 ext. 375

E-mail: info@niot.org

Website: http://www.niot.org/nios

Not in Our School promotes an atmosphere of acceptance and inclusion through videos, activities, and resources to share ways to resist bullying and keep schools safe.

PACER's National Bullying Prevention Center

8161 Normandale Boulevard

Bloomington, MN 55437

(888) 248-0822

E-mail: Bullying411@pacer.org

Website: http://www.pacer.org

PACER provides resources for students, parents, educators, and others to help them recognize bullying and treat it as a serious issue. Its goal is to change the idea that bullying is an accepted part of growing up and instead treat it as a community issue that affects the safety and well-being of school-age youth.

WEBSITES

Because of the changing nature of Internet links, Rosen Publishing has developed an online list of websites related to the subject of this book. This site is updated regularly. Please use this link to access the list:

http://www.rosenlinks.com/411/Bulli

FOR FURTHER READING

Golus, Carrie. *Take a Stand! What You Can Do About Bullying*. Minneapolis, MN: Lerner Publications, 2009.

Hall, Megan Kelley, and Carrie Jones, eds. *Dear Bully: 70 Authors Tell Their Stories*. New York, NY: HarperTeen, 2011.

Hinduja, Sameer, and Justin W. Patchin. *Bullying Beyond the Schoolyard: Preventing and Responding to Cyberbullying*. Thousand Oaks, CA: Corwin Press, 2009.

Jackson, DeSean. *No Bullies in the Huddle*. Dubuque, IA: Kendall Hunt Publishing, 2013.

Jacobs, Thomas A. *Teen Cyberbullying Investigated: Where Do Your Rights End and Consequences Begin?* Minneapolis, MN: Free Spirit Publishing, 2010.

Kilpatrick, Haley, and Whitney Joiner. *The Drama Years: Real Girls Talk About Surviving Middle School—Bullies, Brands, Body Image, and More*. New York, NY: Free Press, 2012.

Kowalski, Robin M., Susan P. Limber, and Patricia W. Agatston. *Cyberbullying: Bullying in the Digital Age*. Malden, MA: Wiley-Blackwell, 2012.

Lohmann, Raychelle Cassada, and Julia V. Taylor. *The Bullying Workbook for Teens*. Oakland, CA: Instant Help, 2013.

Meyer, Stephanie H., John Meyer, Emily Sperber, and
    Heather Alexander. *Bullying Under Attack*. Deerfield
    Beach, FL: Health Communications, 2013.
Nelson, Drew. *Dealing with Cyberbullies*. New York,
    NY: Gareth Stevens Publishing, 2013.
Patchin, Justin, and Sameer Hinduja. *Cyberbullying
    Prevention and Response: Expert Perspectives*. New
    York, NY: Routledge, 2012.
Rivkin, Jennifer. *Physical Bullying*. New York, NY:
    Crabtree Publishing, 2013.
Rivkin, Jennifer. *Social Bullying*. New York, NY:
    Crabtree Publishing, 2013.
Savage, Dan, and Terry Miller, eds. *It Gets Better:
    Coming Out, Overcoming Bullying, and Creating a
    Life Worth Living*. New York, NY: Dutton, 2011.
Simmons, Rachel. *Odd Girl Out, Revised and
    Updated: The Hidden Culture of Aggression in
    Girls*. New York, NY: Mariner Books, 2011.
Stuckey, Rachel. *Cyber Bullying*. New York, NY:
    Crabtree Publishing, 2013.
Subramanian, Mathangi. *Bullying: The Ultimate
    Teen Guide* (It Happened to Me). Lanham, MD:
    Rowman & Littlefield Publishers, 2014.
Swartz, Larry. *The Bully-Go-Round*. Markham, ON,
    Canada: Pembroke Publishers, 2013.
Vanderberg, Hope. *Vicious: True Stories by Teens
    About Bullying*. Minneapolis, MN: Free Spirit
    Publishing, 2012.
Webb, Margaret. *Social Bullying*. New York, NY:
    Crabtree Publishing, 2013.

BIBLIOGRAPHY

Alfano, Sean. "Teens Arrested After Posting YouTube Video of Beating 13-Year-Old Boy and Hanging Him from a Tree." *New York Daily News*, February 1, 2011. Retrieved February 2, 2014 (http://www .nydailynews.com/news/national/teens-arrested -posting-youtube-video-beating-13-year-old-boy -hanging-tree-article-1.137868#ixzz2sCKYtOt7).

American Psychological Association. "Bullying: How Parents, Teachers, and Kids Can Take Action to Prevent Bullying." 2014. Retrieved January 2, 2014 (http://www.apa.org/helpcenter/bullying.aspx).

Berry, Allison. "What Ten Famous Films Teach Us About Bullying." *Time Lists*, September 28, 2011. Retrieved February 1, 2014 (http://content.time .com/time/specials/packages/article/0,28804 ,2095385_2095462_2095500,00.html).

CBC News. "Bullied Student Tickled Pink by Schoolmates' T-shirt Campaign." September 18, 2007. Retrieved February 6, 2014 (http://www.cbc.ca/news/ canada/bullied-student-tickled-pink-by-schoolmates -t-shirt-campaign-1.682221).

CKNW Radio. "Pink Shirt Day." Retrieved February 6, 2014 (http://www.pinkshirtday.ca/about).

CNN Wire. "12-Year-Old Commits Suicide: Girl Accused of Bullying Rebecca Sedwick Has Alibi, Father Says." October 17, 2013. Retrieved January 20, 2014 (http:// www.abc15.com/dpp/news/national/12-year-old

-commits-suicide-girl-accused-of-bullying-rebecca
-sedwick-has-alibi-father-says).

Cohn, Andrea, and Andrea Canter. "Bullying: Facts for
Schools and Parents." National Mental Health and
Education Center for Children and Families Online.
Retrieved December 21, 2013 (http://www.nasponline
.org/resources/factsheets/bullying_fs.aspx).

Coloroso, Barbara. *The Bully, the Bullied, and the
Bystander.* New York, NY: Harper, 2008.

Englander, Elizabeth. *Bullying and Cyberbullying:
What Every Educator Needs to Know.* Cambridge,
MA: Harvard Education Press, 2013.

Fried, SuEllen, and Blanche Sosland. *Banishing
Bullying Behavior: Transforming the Culture of
Peer Abuse.* New York, NY: Rowman & Littlefield
Education, 2011.

Hirsch, Lee, and Cynthia Lowen. *Bully: An Action Plan
for Teachers and Parents to Combat the Bullying
Crisis.* New York, NY: Weinstein Books, 2012.

Kuruvilla, Carol. "Rebecca Sedwick Case: Both Suicide
Victim and Bully Grew Up in 'Disturbing' Family
Environments, Cop Says." *New York Daily News*,
October 25, 2013. Retrieved January 20, 2014
(http://www.nydailynews.com/news/national/
rebecca-sedwick-case-suicide-victim-bully-grew
-disturbing-family-homes-article-1.1496991).

Mason, Kimberly L. *Bullying No More: Understanding
and Preventing Bullying.* Hauppauge, NY: Barron's
Educational Series, 2013.

Patchin, Justin. "Nice It Forward." Cyberbullying Research Center, October 2012. Retrieved February 6, 2014 (http://cyberbullying.us/nice-it-forward).

Rosenberg, Michael. "Sports Can Play a Pivotal Role in Helping Combat Bullying." *Sports Illustrated*, October 6, 2011. Retrieved February 1, 2014 (http://sportsillustrated.cnn.com/2011/writers/michael_rosenberg/10/06/bullying).

Shepherd, Shawna. "White House Conference Tackles Bullying." CNN, March 10, 2011. Retrieved February 18, 2014 (http://www.cnn.com/2011/POLITICS/03/10/obama.bullying).

SaveTeen Rapp. "Bullying and Cyberbullying Facts." SaveTeenRapp.org. Retrieved January 20, 2014 (http://saveteenrapp.org/wp-content/uploads/2012/03/antibully.pdf).

U.S. Department of Health and Human Services. "What Is Bullying?" StopBullying.gov. Retrieved January 8, 2014 (http://www.stopbullying.gov/what-is-bullying/definition/index.html).

WebMD.com. "Domestic Violence—Teen Relationship Abuse." November 17, 2010. Retrieved January 20, 2014 (http://www.webmd.com/mental-health/tc/domestic-violence-teen-relationship-abuse).

YouTube.com. "Nadin Khoury Trailer." JMGProductions, November 13, 2011. Retrieved February 2, 2014 (http://www.youtube.com/watch?v=RByLNIcXZuE).

INDEX

About the Author

Mary-Lane Kamberg is a writer and speaker who specializes in nonfiction for school-age readers. She has written more than twenty books including the titles *Self-Esteem* and *Body Image* and *Teen Pregnancy and Motherhood.*

Photo Credits

Cover, pp. 1, 17 VBStock/iStock/Thinkstock; pp. 4–5 Obama Presidential Campaign/AP Images; p. 9 Reuters/Landov; pp. 10–11 oliveromg/Shutterstock.com; pp. 12–13, 24–25, 84 © AP Images; p. 21 © iStockphoto.com/Christopher Futcher; p. 29 Slyvie Bouchard/Shutterstock.com; p. 33 Mypurgatoryyears/iStock/Thinkstock; p. 36 Creatista/Shutterstock.com; p. 38 Hulton Archive/Getty Images; pp. 40–41 Burger/Phanie/SuperStock; p. 45 FuzzBones/Shutterstock.com; pp. 48–49 Andrzej Wilusz/Shutterstock.com; pp. 52–53 monkeybusinessimages/iStock/Thinkstock; pp. 56–57 Mr Doomits/Shutterstock.com; pp. 60–61 The Washington Post/Getty Images; pp. 62–63 George Doyle/Stockbyte/Thinkstock; p. 67 Mario Tama/Getty Images; pp. 70–71 Liang Sen/Xinhua/Landov; p. 73 Antonio Guillem/Shutterstock.com; pp. 76–77 Portland Press Herald/Getty Images; pp. 82–83 © Bob Ebbesen/Alamy; p. 86 Blend Images/SuperStock; pp. 90–91 David Becker/Getty Images; p. 95 Ovidiu Hrubaru/Shutterstock.com.

Designer: Les Kanturek; Executive Editor: Hope Lourie Killcoyne